The Legend of Kathy Williams

William Kathy Buffalo Soldier

Written by Dr. Gwen Davis

Illustrated by Rasheda Brown

LuLu Publishing Company http://www.lulu.com

The Legend of...

Chapter One

This story begins in a time of trials and tribulations. As you know God will send us through these times to help us become who we are supposed to be. This time of great trials and tribulations was known as slavery.

We were on a farm somewhere in Mississippi, the worst of all the slavery states, when she was born. She was so beautiful. More than a beautiful child, she was as black as the rich earth from which all life springs. And when you gazed in her deep dark eyes there was a spirit that shone all the way back to our glorious days in Egypt.

Her parents Martha and John were captives on a plantation held by the Williams family. The Williams were an evil lot intent on sin and mischief. Martha and John knew they would take their beautiful little girl and commit disgusting crimes upon her even before she was an age of knowledge.

Martha and John knew they had to hide her. To save her from the cruel plans of the evil slave masters Williams. They set up a plan of their own. Martha and John would pretend that their beautiful little girl was really a boy.

It would be simple at first. Martha would not reveal that she had given birth to her beautiful little angel. Every morning before sun up she wrapped heavy cloths around her belly to make it seem like she was still heavy with child. She continued to go to the field and work in the cotton the long hours till sunset. Her back ached and her breasts were heavy with milk, but she could not lie down and nurse her newborn child.

Instead they left the baby with John's sister Ozella. Ozella had had a baby boy just about ten days before Martha gave birth. Everyone was relieved when a boy was born. The boys would be relegated to work their lives away in the cotton fields or the mills. But the little girls would be subjected to such terrible things even before they were the age to work in the fields.

To insure that their crop of babies would not die in the fields, the mothers were always given a month to nurse the babies. So Ozella agreed to suckle both babies in secret.

After a few days of this deception, Martha pretended that she was giving birth. The other women hurried her from the field to the cabin. When the Williams census taker came around to count the children, Martha showed him Ozella boy. He noted the birth as another boy born on the Williams Plantation. The census taker asked, "What you want to call him gal?" "I think we'll call him William after the master if that be alright with you." "That would make the boy known as Will Williams." The census taker muttered under his breath "ignorant niggers" but he noted it down anyway and left. It was agreed upon but in secret they called their little girl Kathy after Martha's mother.

Chapter Two

Now John was the blacksmith on the William's Plantation. He smelted all of the iron work for the farm and he cared for all of the horses and mules. His job was considerable easier than the field hands and he was hardly ever beaten or driven like a mule. In fact his opinion was highly considered when it came to the care and breeding of the fine hot blooded horses he raised for the Williams plantation. They would say Old John he can think like a horse.

He would travel with the Williams boys when they would venture down to New Orleans to trade in horses. They would ask John's opinion as to which horses were best to buy and sell. John's good advice afforded the Williams brothers great fame and wealth from their award winning horses. Because, John was, in fact the best horse doctor and trainer in the whole county.

John had his own little room in the stables with a warm pot belly stove and a real bed. He had a workshop where he prepared the medicines and poultices to keep the horses in fine condition. For a slave he was afforded more freedoms than most. On long nights when all his work was done, he was allowed to walk across the plantation to the slave quarters. John would pick up his wife Martha and their child Kathy. They could visit with him in the stables.

Time passed and all was well with their plan to conceal little Kathy as a boy. They simple dressed the child in boy's clothes and kept her hair cut real short. But Kathy was nearly five years old now and was approaching the age to begin work in the fields.

Martha suggested to John. "The next time you make a good deal for the Williams boys and they are real happy with you, ask them if you can take your own son on in the stable. Tell them you want to coach him to be a good horse doctor. So that when you die they won't go lacking for someone to care for their horses. I'll be willing to bet they'd be selfish enough to take you up on the offer" And so they were and that is how Kathy came to be in her father's care; full time.

Chapter Three

Over the next ten years with her father, Kathy learned everything her dad could teach her. She learned to judge a good horse and how to train one to be an excellent horse. She learned how to heal horses when they were sick or lame. Kathy even learned how to make all the iron works and leather goods for saddles and harnesses. Kathy was a real asset to her father and to the Williams Plantation. No one ever suspected that under those rough and shaggy clothes she was anything but old John's skinny little boy Will.

When Kathy was fifteen, John asked if his boy Will could come along with them to New Orleans to the big horse market. He told the Williams brothers it would be good for little Will to learn about horse trading. John's real intention was that his daughter would get a chance to see the world outside the plantation. He wanted her to learn the roads. Because he wanted more than anything that one day sooner or later his daughter would escape the clutches of slavery. Escape like Harriet Tubman had. Then she could come back one day to rescue them all and carry them away to freedom.

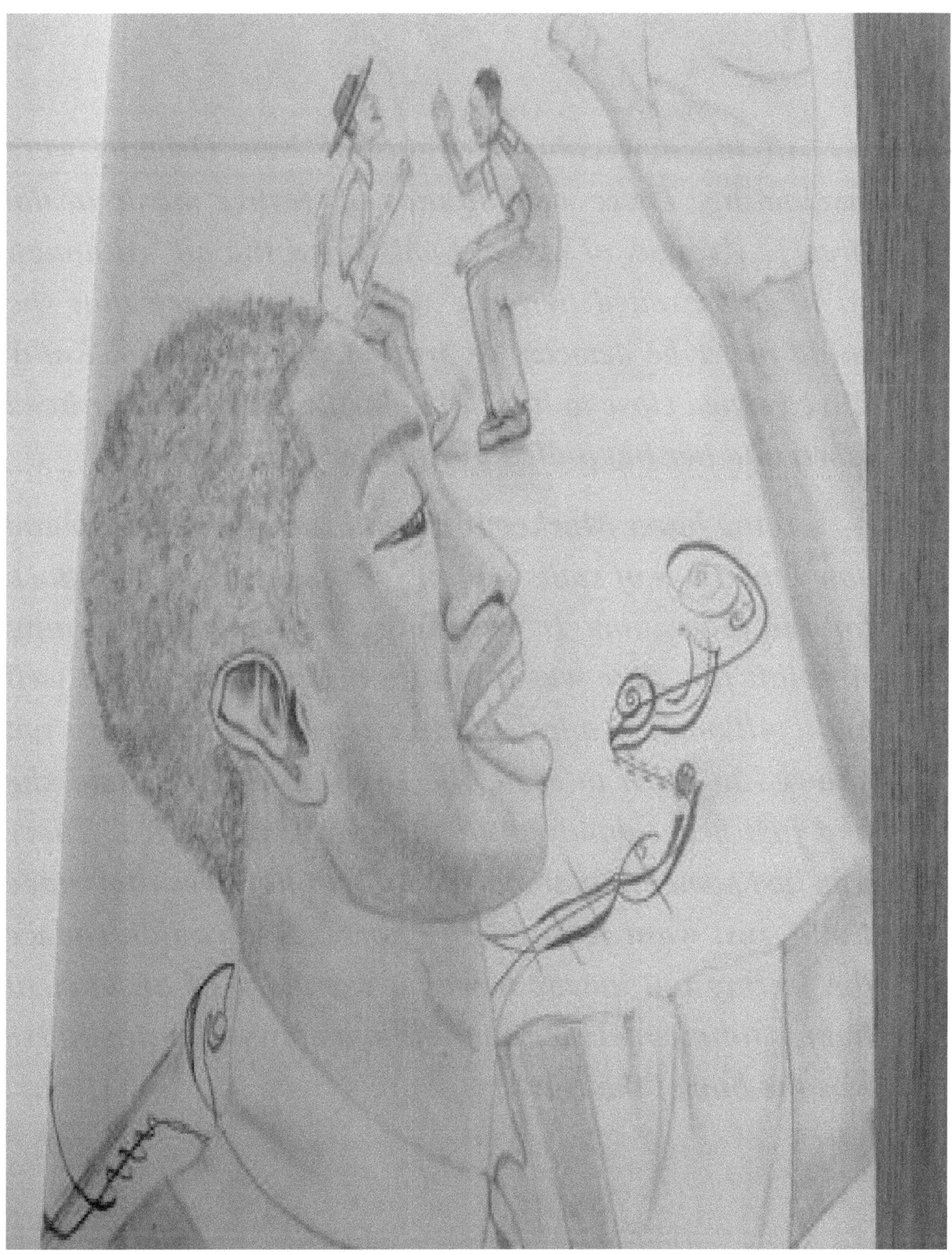

All the new colorful sights of New Orleans were fascinating. There were sounds of festive music in the streets. Aromas of exotic foods filled the air. Although all of this excited her, she was keenly aware that she could never be detected as truly being a girl. So, Kathy stayed glued close to her father's side. She kept her head down and her hat pulled low on her brow.

At the horse Market John and Kathy wander up and down the rows of stalls looking for some fresh new stock for the plantation. It was Kathy who spied the young Arabian filly. She was a blue roan quite small but well built. Although Kathy couldn't read it, slaves were not allowed to learn to read, the sign on her stall said she had just been imported all the way from Africa. There was just something about the look in her eyes that made Kathy just want to know the horse. She couldn't place the feeling but maybe it was a reminder of an ancient home. John convinced the Williams boys that this horse was the buy of the century.

The night times after the trading was all done were the best in New Orleans. The slave masters would go off to the saloons to find liquor, whores and gambling. The Black people held in bondage would be left on their own amongst the rows of livestock stalls. Here free for a while they would seek out each others company. They would share what food they had and the news. Sometimes you could here about a relative that had been sold off to a distant plantation. Sometimes they would sing and clap or play the juice harp. And there was always time to pray. Lately the news was all about Nat Turner and his army of freedom fighters. Rumor had it that General Nat Turner had taken hundreds of Plantations. Freed all the Black people and killed all the white folk. The night in New Orleans was truly full of new things and ideas for Kathy.

At Daylight they left New Orleans with Kathy's little Arab filly and lots of new thoughts in tow.

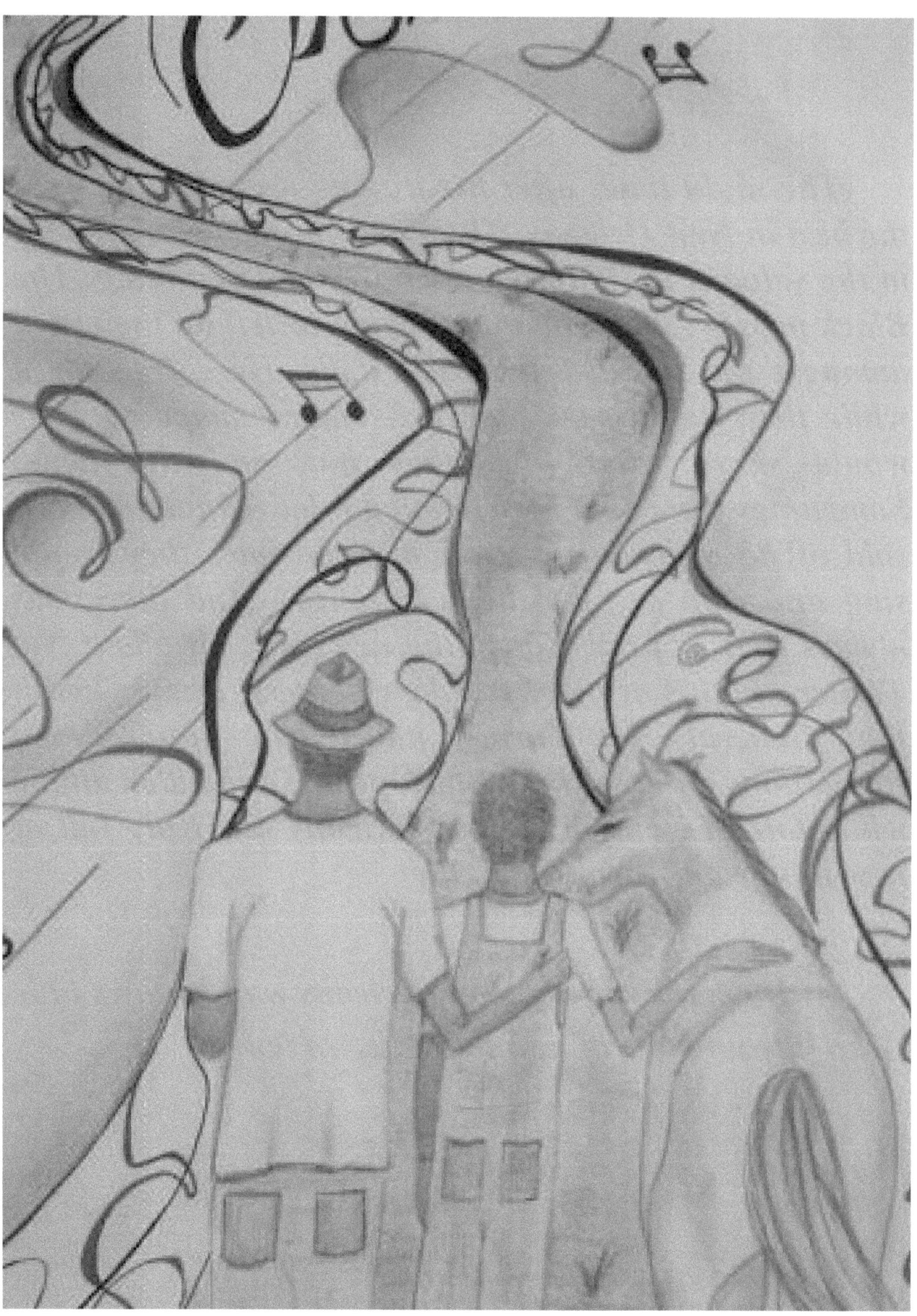

In fact she did turn out to be a great buy because this young filly was already pregnant. No one had noticed that before the sale. So the plantation got two full blooded Arabian horses for the price of one. Kathy named the young filly Ocean because of her blue speckled color and the fact that she had traveled across the ocean from Africa to America.

Chapter Four

Some months later, Ocean gave birth to a strong foal. He was a stallion. He had a dark brown body with a black mane and a black tail and four black stockings. They call that a bey colored horse, like the Sultans of Arabia owned. He looked simple … royal.

This little stallion had a way about him that just longed to be free. He held his head and tail high as he pranced around the pasture. Kathy called him Pride.

John had given over to Kathy the primary duties of training Pride. She had a natural gift for training horses. Every evening after her regular work was finished; she spent hours with the horse. At first just stroking and grooming him to make sure every part of his body was accustomed to her touch. Kathy was always talking to him. In fact, Pride was her only friend. If she got to close to anyone else they may have detected she was really a girl.

Kathy trained Pride to the blanket and the halter, then later to lead on a rope. By the time Pride was two years old she could get him to do anything she wanted. She never even needed to put a bit in his mouth instead she just placed a small thin rope loosely over his head to make him obey. Kathy never whipped Pride. She had seen far too much of that around the plantation. Kathy could get Pride to follow her instructions with a just a little pressure with her legs or a hand gesture. Kathy had trained Pride to ride her easily in five different styles and to jump high obstacles. They were so in tuned to each other that sometimes it looked to John as if the girl could talk to Pride with just her mind.

Chapter Five

Then one evening one of the Williams brothers was out walking around on a heavy drunk. He happened around the back of the stable and saw Kathy riding Pride around the little practice arena. They were a beautiful sight to see. He was surprised and asked John why he had not been told about this prized stallion. John made the excuse that Pride was too small to be bothered with.

John said "Master Williams you would not look stately on such a scrawny little horse he never grew right. He is stunted. That horse won't bring a good price because of his size." Williams protested "He looks so smooth. I just want to try him out."

So Williams strutted out to the little training arena. He grabbed the horse by his lead rope. Kathy quietly dismounted and backed away. Williams grabbed a big hunk of Prides mane and hoisted himself up on Prides back. Pride stood still for just the briefest of seconds then began to buck wildly. He threw Williams down to the ground and trotted over to Kathy.

Williams was outraged. He pulled out the big bullwhip which he always had strapped to his belt. He snapped it wildly making that horrible cracking noise fill the air. Kathy tried to back away with Pride. Williams quickly caught them and began to lash the horse mercilessly cutting into his flesh. Kathy could stand no more and jumped in between the horse and his mad attacker. Williams was shocked by this gesture of selfless compassion. He said "Boy you want to take the beating for the horse then you shall!"

Williams turned his evil whip on Kathy and began to lash her. Williams was viciously practiced with his whip cutting deep wounds into her face and body with every lash. Pride attacked Williams fiercely biting and kicking him. John ran into the arena trying to defend his poor child. Williams was remarkable surprised and then turned the full attention of his whip on his trusted old slave John. On Kathy's cue Pride delivered a full kick with both hind legs straight to Williams head. Blood and brains flew everywhere. Williams was dead.

John was silent for a minute. Then he went to his daughter and hugged her for a long time. It is time now child you will have to go. Take this horse and run. Run to freedom now. Kathy protested "We can explain it. We can tell them it was the horse. That he tried to ride and the horse threw him." John said with a tear in his voice "It won't matter in the least. A Williams is dead and they gonna make somebody pay. At minimum it will be the horse's life and if they get real riled up they may take my life or worse yours."

They left Williams lie where he died whip still clutched in his evil hand.

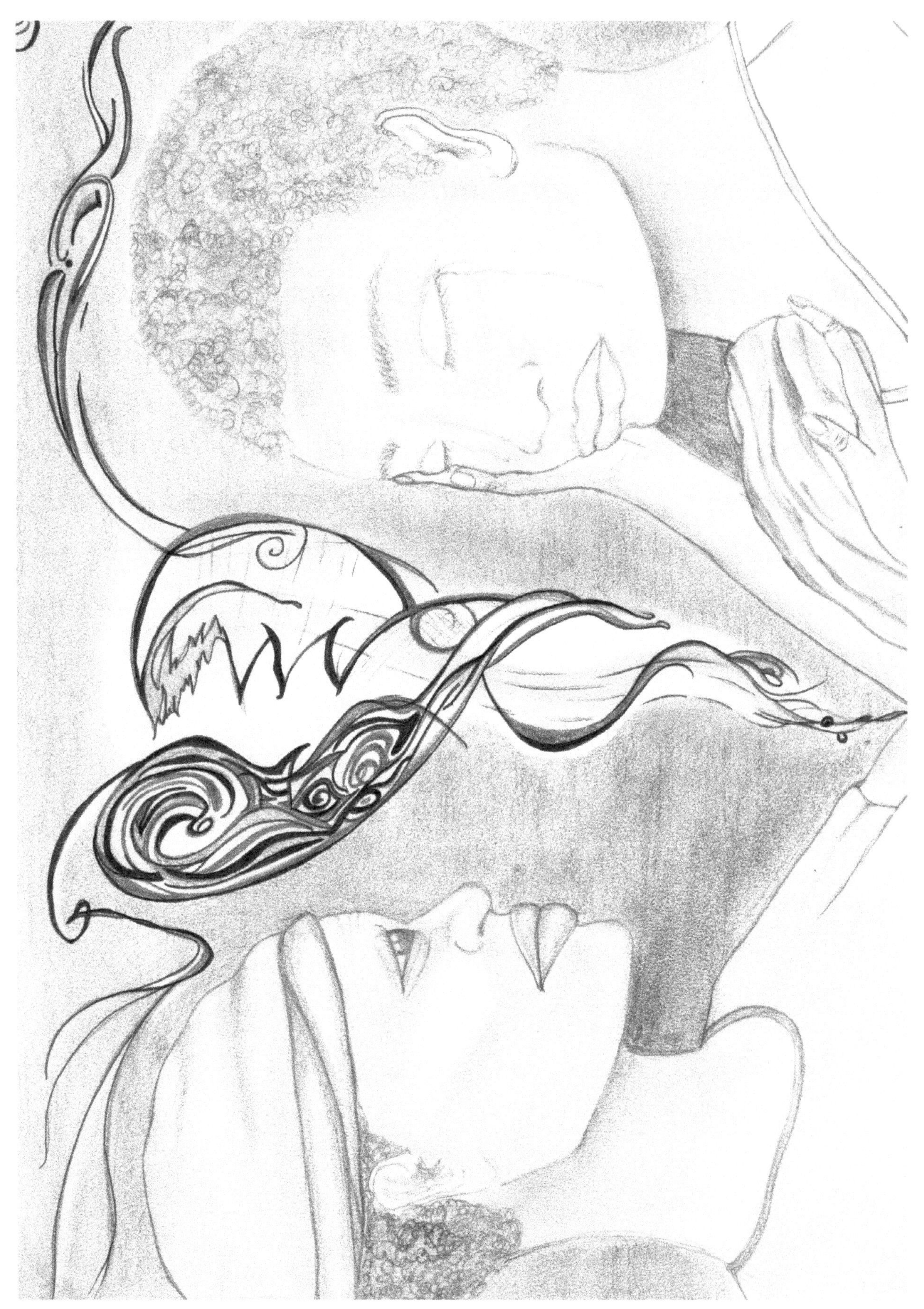

They went straight away to the stable and gathered up some of Kathy's clothes and made a bed roll. When it got dark they headed across the plantation to the slave quarters to find Martha.

Martha was grieved that Kathy had to witness such a terrible things but she knew John was right. Kathy should runaway. The Williams would be looking at everything. They would be looking to close for them to try and keep concealing Kathy's true identity.

Martha held John and Kathy's hands and said a prayer. Then before the prayer was over she knew exactly what to do.

"Here Kathy take this dress and this head scarf too and put it in your bed roll." Kathy said "But I never even wore a dress before. I don't know how." Her Mother replied "It ain't hard child. Just slip it on. You are going to have to dress like a girl now. They won't look for you at first but after the crying dies down the Williams are going to notice you are gone.

But they will be looking for a boy not a young woman. Take the little horse and travel by night on the horse. In the day time lead the horse, dressed as a woman. If anyone stops you say you are delivering the horse to the livestock sale in New Orleans for the Smith plantation. Then you travel west all the way. Ask any Black folks where General Nat Turner is camped now. Maybe you can join up with the freedom fighters. You could be of some help to them, knowing all what you have learned about horses. John you go back to the stable and put one of your meanest horses in that arena with Williams body. Then go straight to your room and try to sleep." Martha having finished explaining her plan kissed her daughter goodbye and said ride with God's speed.

Chapter Six

Kathy rode hard through the night following the roads to New Orleans. By day break Pride was lathered a tired. She stopped by a stream to cool him down and give him water. They both refreshed themselves in the stream. Then Kathy founds some herbs to make a soothing suave for the lash wounds on both of their bodies. They rested there by the stream for a long while. Pride ate the fresh grass and Kathy found some good roots and berries. They moved into the forest even further away from the road. Kathy pulled out her bed roll and lied down for some much needed sleep. Pride laid down right next to her. They both slept through the day.

The pair continued west that night. Each day they rested. Each night they traveled. In just a few days without really seeing anyone on the way they arrived in New Orleans. They arrived very late in the night and just rode right into town. It was the same busy city Kathy had remembered. She went relatively unnoticed as it was not all that unusual to see a free Black man in New Orleans.

She headed straight for the market and the relative safety of the horse trading stalls. She dismounted and began to walk the rows of horse stalls. Pride followed right on her heals without being tethered. She finally came upon a group of sleepy Black folk. They were all hunkered down and dosing but not really sleep. Most folks didn't really want to spend their free night in the quarters sleeping. Kathy sat down with them and in her deepest voice introduced herself as little Will. A fat molatto fellow handed Will a piece of sweet corn bread and said "Good to meet you Will. Where you hail from?" Will said "Thank You much sir I sure am hungry. But it don't matter where I hail from. What matters is where I'm going." "Oh, I sees. Where are you going then young Will?" "To tell the truth, I am looking for General Nat Turner to join up with the freedom fighters." "Is that right boy then you are a mighty brave young man." "Do you know where I can find Nat Turner and his army?" "No I rightly don't. But I wish I did. Cause if I did I get this fat body right up from here and join you."

Just then another soul spoke up from the darkness. "I hear that all that talk about Nat Turner just ain't so. I hear told it is all just a rumor." That comment sparked a lot of talk and several more folks joined into the chatter. Some adamantly believed in General Nat Turner and others were sure it wasn't so and others just couldn't make up their mind. Finally one old dark man who seemed as old and as wise as Methuselah himself said "Now look here all of you. Oh course, Nat Turner is real and God done sent him to free us all. And if this boy wants to find him and join him he will. The old man turned to Little Will and said. "Get some rest boy and in the morning, you head right on out of town. Go west. And don't stop till you find what you are looking for. Another man said "Yes, I came here from a plantation on out west. I was in the back of the master's wagon but I clearly saw a group of soldiers camped just out of town. They was wearing blue uniforms all of them and I do swear before God all of them soldiers had black faces as black as you and I. I didn't understand it but master just drove the wagon on by.

If that was Nat Turner's Freedom fighters I reckon Master was just scared to say anything." Kathy laid out her bed roll right there and Pride lay down with her. They rested but they couldn't sleep.

Chapter Seven

In the morning the market was very busy. The people she had spoken with so freely during the night were now jumping to the commands of their captures. People and horses were moving in all directions. Kathy hid in an empty stall and quickly changed into the dress and scarf her mother had provided. Kathy knew it was time to be just a slave woman delivering a horse. That disguise did work. Kathy had quietly maneuvered through the crowd and was almost clear of the Market. Then a guard asked, "Where is your sales paper gal?" Kathy said "Sir I don't have no paper." "Well then Gal you going to have to walk way back cross the Market and ask your Master to give it to you. Cause I have to see it before you can exit the Market."

Kathy didn't think going back was a real option. She knew west was where she wanted to go. And she believed Nat Turners men where camped right out side of town. So she stepped back hiked up her dress and leaped on Pride with one bound. She took off with such speed that it knocked the guard right off his feet.

It took quite a few minutes for the guard to gather his senses. Then he had to round up some men to chase the woman. Whom he believed was a common horse thief. By then Pride had easily run five miles ahead of their pursuers. Pride and Kathy ran at a full gallop all the way out of town. They ran at a thundering pace praying all the way that they would soon encounter the safety of General Nat Turner's troop. Then in the distance like a dream come true was the answer to their prayers.

It was the camp straight ahead just a few miles. There was a perimeter erected from wood about four feet high completely surrounding the camp. There was only one entry gate and one exit to the rear. There were tents lined in rows. There were horses tethered and ready for action. There was a full troop of blue suited soldiers just ahead. As she rode closer she could see the soldiers guarding the entrance to the camp.

The soldiers could see her coming also. In fact she was causing a great deal of alarm in the camp. Sergeant the guard yelled. "There is a rider coming really fast. I can't be sure from that distance but I think it is a woman." The sergeant approached the perimeter. He used his telescope to get a better look. "You may be right soldier, who ever it is they are coming mighty fast. Stay ready." The soldiers readied their rifles. As she got closer Kathy could see the faces of the soldiers and she knew they were defiantly Black men. She began to yell out loud "Please, Don't shoot I am a Black man too and I have come to join you freedom fighters!" The sergeant reluctantly said "Hold your fire." By then Kathy and Pride were right upon them. She didn't stop she never even slowed down. Kathy simply gave Pride a silent command and jumped the four foot wall right into the camp. The soldiers tried in vain to stop her but she eluded them with ease. Pride danced all around them as if they were moving in slow motion. The sergeant yelled to his men beware this is no woman. "It is someone only dressed as a woman. I don't think there is a woman on earth that can ride like that."

Kathy finally stopped Pride right in front of the sergeant because by his commanding aura she knew he was in charge. Kathy dismounted and knelt in front of the sergeant. "Sir, is you General Nat Turner?" The sergeant could hardly contain his amusement. "No, I am not. I am Sergeant Dan Plair of the ninth US Calvary Buffalo soldier. Who are you?" She replied again in her deepest voice. "My name is William... William Kathy and I have come to join the freedom fighters. Sergeant Plair looked Kathy up and down real hard. "And why young man, are you wearing your mothers dress?" "Sir, it is only a disguise to hide from the slave masters. Young William pulled off the head scarf revealing her closely cropped hair. "See, I am a man."

Just then the gate guard called out again to the sergeant. "More riders approaching fast." Again the sergeant peered through his telescope. This time he saw it was a group of white men. They were most certainly a posse after the youth. The sergeant didn't hesitate. "Hide him!" the soldiers led young William to a tent. Pride followed right behind and they both hunkered down low inside the tent as quiet as church mice.

The men arrogantly approached the Black soldiers guarding the camp. "We want to come in and look for a horse thief." The guard calmly replied. "Sorry but you can not come in here this is a US military camp." The white man spat on the ground. "Military camp my ass, all I see is a bunch of niggers." Eight more soldiers join the guards at the gate. Each one holding their rifles ready to fire. The guard spoke very calmly. "This is my second warning. If you try to enter this US military camp you will be shot… dead." With that cold response the posse backed off. They just decided their lives were worth more than catching one horse stealing woman.

In time Sergeant Plair gave the order for William to come out of hiding. They were both a mess. Pride was muddy and covered in sweat. William had removed the dress but his boy clothes were tattered and covered with dirt. The lash scars were real evident on both of them. The sergeant said. "The both of you look like you been through hell and back. Are you sure you want to join up with us." Kathy asked "Are you with General Nat Turner's army of freedom fighters" The sergeant said "No, I told you we are the United States ninth Calvary. But I guess you could call us freedom fighters. We serve under President Abraham Lincoln and he has promised to put an end to slavery. Kathy said "I am not so sure. My mother told me to find General Nat Turner do you know where he is?" "No, son I don't. But I think your mother would be just as proud if you became one of us a Buffalo Soldier.

So, that is how Kathy Williams...William Kathy became a Buffalo Soldier. She served as a man in the US Calvary for more than twenty years. When she retired she moved to Colorado. Many nights around the campfire she told the children about her adventures as a Buffalo Soldier.

And Grandma Gwen knows them all.

Next read

The Adventures of

William Kathy…Kathy Williams

Buffalo Soldier

www.ingramcontent.com/pod-product-compliance
Ingram Content Group UK Ltd.
Pitfield, Milton Keynes, MK11 3LW, UK
UKHW051134260726
13967UKWH00010B/3037